Test Your Color

Test Your Color

Test Your Color

Test Your Color

Test Your Color

Test Your Color

Test Your Color

Test Your Color

Test Your Color

Test Your Color

Test Your Color

Test Your Color

Test Your Color

Test Your Color

Test Your Color

Test Your Color

Test Your Color

Test Your Color

Test Your Color

Test Your Color

Test Your Color

Test Your Color

Test Your Color

Test Your Color

Test Your Color

Test Your Color

Test Your Color

Test Your Color

Test Your Color

Test Your Color

CPSIA information can be obtained
at www.ICGtesting.com
Printed in the USA
LVHW061000210123
737671LV00031B/1003